BY THE SAME AUTHOR

(Published by the Somesuch Press)

The Case of the Missing Umlaut
The Unwritten Tales of Annabelle Nevvers
(2 vols.)

FROM BEOWULF TO VIRGINIA WOOLF

A LITERARY MAP
OF ENGLAND
Boswell Field
Silver Sea
Wed Loch
Yale Loch
Rape Loch
Loch Slee Hall
Rin-Tin-Tin's Abbey
The Hence of Forth
Northanger Abbey
Prentice Hall
Fingal's Cave
McGraw Hill
Longman's Green
Heathcliff
Free Aire
Wordsworthshire
Lake Eerie
Upsom Downs
Third Forth
Mazefield
Burnt Gidding
Aire
The Puritan Interlude
Upper Plate over Stourbridge
Some Bridge
Um Bridge
The Slot
Bard-on-Avon
Sussex
Nossex
Pepys' Dairy
Middlesex
Tono Bungay
Lady Windermere's Farm
Raspberry Hill
Stoke Penge
Suffix
Drake's Bowling Alley
Parade's End

From Beowulf to Virginia Woolf

An Astounding and Wholly Unauthorized History of English Literature

by

ROBERT MANSON MYERS, Ph.D. (Oxen)

THE BOBBS-MERRILL COMPANY, INC.
Publishers
Indianapolis New York

Printed in the United States of America

First Edition

NOTE

From Beowulf to Virginia Woolf was first published in the Spring 1951 issue of *Furioso,* from which it is here reprinted (in slightly altered form) by kind permission of the editors. Acknowledgment is made to The Viking Press, Inc., for their permission to adapt several of the boners in their series of *Boners* books (very recently augmented by *Bigger and Better Boners*) for inclusion in this volume. Acknowledgment is also made to The Macmillan Company for their permission to reproduce illustrations from *A Book of English Literature, Volume I: from Beowulf to William Blake,* edited by Franklyn Bliss Snyder and Robert Grant Martin; and to The Houghton Mifflin Company for their permission to reproduce illustrations from *The History of the Novel in England,* by Robert Morss Lovett and Helen Sard Hughes.

To

MY FATHER AND MOTHER

Who Made All This Possible

Foreword

The present study grew out of a doctoral disputation written at a fashionable eastern finishing school; it appears now only after years of expensive revision and diligent research at the Harvard Theological Cemetery and the British Mausoleum. Grateful acknowledgment is hereby extended to my wife, who has requested that I withhold her name from the Index.

R. M. M.

Contents

List of Illustrations

FROM BEOWULF TO VIRGINIA WOOLF

CHAPTER ONE

The Wolf at the Door

Who's afraid of the big Beowulf?
—Olde Anguische Carol

At the door of English literature stands Beowulf, the great Dane, who once upon a time inhabited the forest primeval with Ethelwulf, his wife, and is therefore known as "The Noble Savage." It would, of course, be absurd to dwell on Beowulf's particulars in a brief survey such as this, especially since those details are fully recorded in Beowulf's autobiographical beast epic, first published in 1066 as *The Doomsday Book.* This famous first edition was printed on a cotton manuscript, destroyed by fire in 1731 and later purchased from descendants of the Beowulf family by Andrew Carnegie. The original duodecimo is totally ineligible. With the persistent efforts of scholars, however, it has emerged that Beowulf sailed forth boldly into the filth and froth of the Firth of Forth in the spring of 596. Following his slaughter of Grendel (a task as odious as Oedipus' cleansing of the Aegean stables), the epic hero retraced his footsteps across the sea. His spritely narrative abounds with sketches of such Cro-Magnon dignitaries as Half-Dane, High-Shellac and Wroth-Child.

Since England is located on the coast of Great Britain and therefore not far from the sea, she has always been subject to continental influences. Christianity was introduced by the Romans in 55 B.C., and it was not long before England was overrun by Angels, Sextons and Jukes, who settled north of the Humber River near the Ooze. The Angels and Sextons were superstitious people who still worshiped ghosts, goblins, virgins and other supernatural monsters, but the Jukes followed the so-called Saline Law, according to which:

(1) no man could be king if descended from a woman; and (2) one must take everything with a grain of salt.

Despite such laws the English throne continued to thrive, and the line of English kings accordingly includes such names as Old King Cole, the Little Lame Prince and the King of the Golden River. In order to stimulate the production of ballads, epics and literature Old King Cole passed the Danelaw, the Poor Law and the Ancren Rule, and in order to encourage the creation of sagas he himself, although unmarried at the time, translated the *Gretchensaga* into Olde Anguische.

Later Cynewulf, a Medium High German monk of St. Edmunds, produced *The Dream of the Rude*, an ill-punctuated diatribe in Olde Norse. Subsequent criticism of Cynewulf's doggerel caused the rise of a fierce motto: "Bury St. Edmunds" (presumably alive). Cynewulf had been a pupil of the Venerable Bede, the Wolfsbane. In his *Two Years Before the Mass* Bede explained how, as author of the Catholic *Missile,* he entered a monastery and in two years became the father of English literature.

ZARATHUSTRA
King Arthur's Columbine
From a unanimous source

Frequently Olde Anguische verse was translated into Gnomic and recited by barges who traveled about the country. Such verse was rugged, unkempt and usually marked by Caesarean pause. Its two chief exponents were Ethelred the Unread, son of Eveready the Red and Ethel the Unready, and St. Wulfstan Wulfilas, a Goth who, beholding a moat in his brother's eye, translated the Bible into Gothic.

If the Venerable Bede was the father of English literature, then certainly Alfred the Great was its oldest son. In early youth Alfred founded *The Anglo-Saxon Chronicle,* the first English mouth organ, which continued on and off for more than two centuries. His chief significance, however, lies in his nephew King Arthur, who married the Lady of Shalott and thereupon founded the Order of the Knights of the Wife of Bath. Tales of adventure, especially in Arabia, were nightly related to King Arthur at the Crystal Palace by Zarathustra, one of his columbines, who seduced him with stories of Sin the Bad Sailor and the Four Horsemen of the Acropolis. At King Arthur's round-table discussions gathered the Idols of the King, and there one might have beheld such Idols as Launcelot, Excalibur, Childe Roland and, of course, the page boy Bob.

CHAPTER TWO

The Big Bad Wolf

Pox vobiscum.
—Muddle Latin Proverb

Time before 1066 is now reckoned as "Time In Memoriam." In that year William the Conqueror and his merry men defeated Childe Harold at the Battle of Hastings, ruthlessly raised London to the ground and immediately passed an edict forbidding all births, marriages and deaths in England for a period of one year. William was, according to his usual custom, killed in battle. Before his death, however, he was forced to sign the Magna Carta, a famous document providing that: (1) no man should be imprisoned for debt so long as he had the money to pay; and (2) no free man should be hanged twice for the same offense.

Later William established the Futile System, with its intricate relationships between lord, vessel, serf and villain. His greatest contribution, of course, was the Guilt System, an organization designed to encourage arts and graft. It was England's foremost guild, the Early English Textile Society, that drew up the Mosaic Code, according to which medevil mosaic workers were permitted to send their children to the Merchant Sailors Mysteries.

In 878 Alfred the Great had passed the so-called "Grim" Law, according to which Olde Anguische was to be superseded in 1066 by Muddle English. Thus overnight the language and literature of England passed from infancy to adultery, with three genders (masculine, feline and neutral), eight parts of speech (nouns, pronouns, adjectives, propositions, verbs, adverbs, proverbs and irregular verbs), and three cases (nominal, genital and ablaut). And as a result of the Great Germanic Sound-Split, Ancient Illyrian *x* became Indo-Iranian *y* except when preceded by a penultimate ablative obsolete.

WILLIAM THE CONQUEROR

"His greatest contribution . . . was the Guilt System."

From a mosaic by the Early English Textile Society

Against this frightful background Muddle English literature sprang up and even flourished. The Muddle Ages were fond of romance, and English writers, following the example of the Old High German *minnowsingers,* enrolled at the New School of Courtly Love in London and produced courtly tales now known as *chanson de beau geste.* The typical medevil *chanson* presents a succession of nightly adventures, loosely related in French polysyllabic couplets.

Of the four great Middle Aged poets (Chaucer, Gore, Pearl the Poet, and the Peerless Plowman) Chaucer was the first who dared forsake the classic Latin of his father to write in his mother's tongue. In early youth Chaucer commenced *The Canterbury Tales,* a parchment of fools based on Boccaccio's *Consolation of Boethius* (a collection of fourteenth-century pornographs). In 1066 an exasperating archbishop named St. Thomas Aquinas had acquired an extraordinary reputation for holiness after being murdered by T. S. Eliot in Canterbury Cathedral. Chaucer's Canterbury Pilgrims, best known as the Prodigal Fathers, relate colorful episodes of marriage as they make their annual Pilgrim's Progress to St. Thomas' Canterbury shrine.

About this time Pearl the Poet, presumably female and therefore probably a nun, wrote *Sir Gawain and the Green Girdle,* in which she related how Sir Gawain, the Green Knight, was first beknighted and, adorning his coat of male, departed upon his *horse de combat* in quest of the Holy Grail. Other pious poets of the period include the Peerless Plowman, author of *The Vision of Sir Launfal,* and John Gore, the Black Death, who met a gruesome end when he was excommunicated by a papal bull.

During the Muddle Ages monks and nuns lived in a state of unbridled celibacy. Finding the Seven Cardinal Sins more engaging than the Seven Deadly Virtues, such monks as John the Gaunt and Charles the Bald lived according to *The Anglican Rule* in constant communion with St. Thomas More, St. Thomas Browne, St. Thomas Beecham and sundry others of the clerical choler. While Abou Ben Adhem chanted "Gloria in Excelsior" to Charlie the Chaplain and Edward the Confessor, St. Vincent Millay, clad

MAHATMA DANTE
Chief among medevil dramatists, author of
The Divine Comedy
From the Pre-Raphaelite Collection

in coat of alms, helped Monk Lewis found the Order of the Grey Friers. Medevil religious zeal was further expressed by John Wycliff (of Dover), who exhausted thousands of sinners to repentance. But when Wycliff translated the Old Testament into the New, he was condemned as hereditary and burned as a steak. Following his death several "University Wits" instigated the so-called Pedant's Revolt, upon which occasion Henry VI Part III made his astute observation: "The pedants are revolting."

Religious fanaticism found expression also in medevil philosophy and drama. St. Thomas Aquinas' treatment of logic, ethics and ascetics in *Summa Theologica* is the crowning achievement of Muddle Latin literature. In discussing Apostolic Secession, St. Thomas (a monist) and Dunce Scotus (a duelist) caused much hare-splitting over the question of how many angels could dance at once on pins and needles.

Such debates appeared frequently in the mystery plays, miracle plays and other dumb shows of the period. Chief among medevil dramatists was Mahatma Dante, whose *Divine Comedy* has become the favorite farce of all time. In three acts ("Hell," "Purgatory" and "Heaven") Dante described his love for Beatrice, the Blessed Damozel, revealing how he secured permission to go to hell, and how upon his arrival he found Beatrice out on a limbo. Living in the fourteenth century, Dante was at once a pre-Raphaelite and a forerunner of the Renaissance. He stood with one foot in the Muddle Ages, while with the other he hailed the dawn of a new day.

CHAPTER THREE

Wolf-Gathering

A wolf's a wolf for a' that.
—Burns

That literary period which lapsed from Chaucer to Shakespeare is now known as the Baron Period of English culture, since barons who were not themselves barren married baronesses who were, of course, especially barren. Throughout those Dark Ages England was known as the Dark Continent. Wolf-hunting had been a favorite pastime of the ancient Britons, but England, now wolfless, forsook Beowulf and Cynewulf for the saner joys of the printing press, the wine press and John Skeleton, whose ghastly *Skeleton in*

Armor is the only incunabulum now in the closet of the East Bronx Public Library.

Most familiar to the specialist of fifteenth-century literature is the popular ballad. Two types of ballads, both of French origin, dominated the late Muddle English literary scene: the *ballet doux* and the *ballet ruse*. Each was a form of anesthetic dancing, and each employed such devices as mnenotony, schenectady, illiteration and eternal rhyme. Such great ballads as "The Fox and the Wolf" and "Little Red Robin Hood," by Wolfhound von Eschenbach, an extremely Low German of the fifteenth century, immediately suggest "Barbarous Allen," "Kemp Malone" and other cuckoo songs by Old Mother Goose, author of "The Golden Egg." Even more brilliant is Thomas Rhymer's "Owl and Florence Nightingale," a satire on crows, pigeons and other eavesdroppers.

During the fifteenth century Italy was ruled by Machiavelli, the Black Prince. Skilled in all forms of arts and craft, Machiavelli believed that Virgil is its own reward. Accordingly he promoted the study of Sophocles, Aristotle and Pluto, and later he built the Painter's Palace of Pleasure to house masterpieces of Renaissance art. There one might have beheld the splendor of Archipelago's murals (now on the dome of the Sistine Madonna), or the even more striking portraits of Rubens, whose keen interest in the female nude led him to be known as the father of the Renaissance. When one remembers the canvases of Andrea del Sarto, a designer of women whose reach unfortunately exceeded his grasp, one instantly recalls Fra Flippo Flippi, whose "Adoration of Virgil" is surpassed only by Fra Michael Angelico's "Jewels of the Madonna."

About this time Martin Luther was arrested for selling indulgences on the streets of Rome without a license. For his doctoral degree this German scholar had written ninety-five theses (with footnotes), none of which had been published but all of which had been foolishly tacked on the doors of Wittenberg Cathedral. Provoked by this *ex-cathedral* defiance of Cannon Law, Pope Pontifex IX instantly excommunicated Luther from the Holy Roman Empire. But Luther girded his lions and deified the Pope. After a Diet of Bologna and a Diet of Worms he was naturally eager for a Reformation, and, filled with riotous indignation, he slew the papal bull and proclaimed his doctrine of transubstantiation by faith.

In the light of the Italian Renaissance and the Protestant Revolt, England found it wise to choose a house of a different color. Accordingly Henry VIII (Prince Hal) was given full reign, and at the suggestion of his prime minister, Oliver Cromwell, he immediately proclaimed himself "Offender of the Faith." Eventually Henry divorced Katharine the Great in order to marry Lady Zane Grey, whose father thereupon wrote his elegy in a country churchyard.

Throughout the Muddle Ages England had been Roman Catholic, but with Henry's divorce she became Christian, although the French still obstinately believed in God and remained Catholic. Sacred matters grew more complex with Bloody Mary, whose zeal for roasting Protestants caused her brief reign to be known as the "Shorter Cataclysm." A distinct tone of unrest naturally pervades Tottel's *Miscellany*, which introduced the euphemisms of John Lyly and the Italian sonnets of Plutarch.

Meanwhile, Christopher Columbus had sailed the ocean blue in search of the United

THE INVISIBLE SPANISH ARMADA

States. Incensed, Queen Elizabeth demanded that English explorers at once circumnavigate the known universe. More incensed, Philip II of Spain sought to invade England with his Invisible Armada, but Sir Francis Drake spied them out while bowling and cried, "A sail! A sail!" Philip's defeat by Captain Kydd is now known as *The Spanish Tragedy; or, Fifty Thousand Colleagues under the Sea.*

CHAPTER FOUR

The She-Wolf

The specious times of great Elizabeth.
—Tennyson

Growth of literary activity in Elizabethan England caused Elizabeth to be known as "The Virgin Queen." As a queen she was highly successful. Clever and beautiful, with red hair and freckles, she was also wise and virtuous, and therefore she never married but instead swore like a sailor and painted herself and other things. Often she threw her spinsterhood into the sea of European politics, and, though neither Roman nor Catholic, she more than once threatened to execute all those who would not swear that she was the Pope.

She was so fond of dresses that she was seldom seen without one on. One day, however, when she rode through Coventry with *nothing* on, Sir Walter Scott offered her his velvet cloak, upon which occasion Edmund Spenser dedicated to Elizabeth his masterpiece, *The Virgin Queene.* Although only six of the twelve proposed cantos of this poem have survived, Dr. Johnson's comment is still final: "Sir," he once declared (breathing through his diagram), "one should dispense with any dispenser of Spenser."

In order to appreciate Elizabethan drama one must first understand fully the Greek drama of the Age of Pericles. Following the victory of Thesaurus at the Battle of Salami (one of Caesar's Pubic Wars), three Greek tragedians (Aeschylus, Socrates and Euripides) settled near the Delphic Oracle (a volcano giving amphibious answers) to produce classical tragedy. According to Aristotle, "Tragedy is a purgative of the emotions through piety and fear, with the kathartics of these." In classical tragedy all action occurs offstage. Following this difficult restriction, Socrates wrote such terrible tragedies as *Electron* and *The Trichinae,* both based on his well-known philosophy that "No man knows anything." Socrates was a Stoic (a disciple of Zero) who thought of himself as a fly sent to gad about Athens, but unfortunately he was also a heavy drinker, and in time hemlock corrupted his morals.

It was to the Greeks and Romans that Elizabethan dramatists looked for guidance in their early tragedies, most of which revolt against the conventions of Middle Age. The greatest Elizabethan playwright was Christopher Morley, a truly first-rate dramatist but for Shakespeare. In *Doctor Faustus* Morley's tragic flaw was his failure to divide his play into acts and scenes. For this fatal blunder he was never forgiven by Frances Bacon, a sister of Roger Bacon and the only reputable female writer of the period. Bacon founded *The Atlantic Monthly* and originated the modern system of Inductive Thinking known as Bacon's Rebellion. Until recently the so-called Shakespeare-Bacon controversy remained a mute question, but it has finally been established,

SHAKESPEARE WITH BACON

An oppressed picture recently excavated by the extinguished scholar, Dr. Piddle. (This photograph is sometimes erroneously terminated "The Other Shakespeare.")

after the perusal of a rare manuscript found in a bottle, that Shakespeare never wrote Shakespeare's plays. Actually they were written by another man of the same name.

William Shakespeare was the greatest dramatist the world has yet to produce. He came of a very respectable family and was, through no fault of his own, born in 1564 near Suffix, England. In extreme youth he settled at Windsor with his eight merry wives, where he remained until 1611, when he removed to Stratford-on-Auburn, more commonly known as the Deserted Village. Shakespeare is famous today chiefly for his plays, most of which have, unfortunately, been dramatized. As a child he wrote *Love's Labour's Lust,* to be followed shortly by *As You Lack It* (a high comedy), *The Merchant of Venus* (a low comedy) and *Anatomy and Coleoptera* (a comedy of errors). It is by his tragedies, however, that he is generally distinguished. Inspired by the works of Seneca, a Roman prefix under Emperor Trojan, Shakespeare's tragedies appear in blank verse (unrhymed ironic pentameter) and usually present a fool (sometimes Shakespeare himself). Best known are *Othello* (the first domestic tragedy), *King Lear* (the last domestic tragedy) and *Hamlet* (a Danish tragedy).

After her death in 1603 Queen Elizabeth graciously relinquished her throne to James I, reputed to be "the wildest fool in Christendom." James believed in the Divine Rite of Kings, and after writing the St. James Bible he became known as "Author and Finisher of the Faith."

The St. James Version of the Bible has been called "the noblest monument of English prose." A glance at Bartlett's *Familiar Quotations* reveals how many Bibulous passages have become part of our daily speech. In the Five Books of Moses, written on the famous Twelve Tables, we learn how Cain raised cane against Abel, how Jacob (son of Aesop) stole his brother's birthmark, and how Moses led the children of Egypt into the Promised Land of Canada. It was on this memorable journey that Lot's wife was sent into the desert to become a pillar of salt by day and a pillar of fire by night. Shortly thereafter we read how David the Psalmist married the Queen of

Bathsheba and became the father of Solomon and Gomorrah, how Jonah the Whale swallowed Jude the Obscure, and how Elijah abandoned Elisha, his wife, to go on a cruise with a widow.

CHAPTER FIVE

The Lone Wolf

Sunday is icumen in:
Lewdly sing cuckoo!
—Puritan Motto

When Charles I, the Spanish Cavalier, descended to the English throne in 1625 he determined to prove his piety by stamping out all religion in England. Acting upon the advice of Archbishop Lawd, who was deeply religious and therefore obstinate and untruthful, he summoned all Puritans, Cavilists, Morons, Drunkards and other Nonconformists and "hurried them out of the land." Later, when the Long Parliament finally dissolved into the Parliament of Fools, Charles I summoned the celebrated Rumpus Parliament, after which he was beheaded, declared unconstitutional, sold into government bonds and speedily exisled.

Among the leaders of the so-called Puritan Interlewd, John Stuart Milton (the Last Puritan) was a poet of epic-making importance and one of the millstones of English literature. He was to the manor born. After choosing poetry as his vacation, he secured a poetic license and embarked upon the threshold of a literary career.

Milton was a poet in all five senses, but he was sometimes deficient in taste. In "Lycidas" he mourned the death of his friend, King Edward, through the allegorical disguise of St. Peter and Ole Man River. In his "Sonnet on His Third Birthday," which is indeed neither sonnet nor sequence, he followed the form of the Italian (Plutarchan) sonnet rhyming, *alibabacededegg*. The triumph of his early years, however, came with "Ill Spenseroso," a piece of Spenserian criticism in Italian anapestilent tetrimeter.

Milton's prose tends to be dull and monogamous, and his verse is almost totally blank. But in *Areopagitica,* modeled on Cicero's ovations to Catiline, Milton's conception of liberty

THE GRATE FIRE OF LONDON

From an old carbon

becomes most striking: "I cannot praise a fugitive and cloistered virgin, unexorcised and unbreathed, that never sallies out and sees her adversary, but slinks out of the race." In the light of these lines Milton's marriage to Mary Powell assumes the greatest impotence.

In his blindness Milton produced his most imperishable creation, *Paradox Lost,* which, although not a sonnet, is an admirable piece of verse and one of the best-punctuated poems in English. Like the epics of Homer, Virgil and other epicures, *Paradox Lost* takes its inspiration from Holy Wit. For a scholarly appraisal of Eve's Temptation, Stumble and Fall one should consult Keats' "Eve and St. Agnes," which pictures Ariel (an acute angel) and Uriel (an obtuse angel) at the precise moment when Eve, gazing on Satan with wild-eyed amusement, plucks Adam's apple.

Before the publication of *Paradox Lost* the Puritan Interlewd had ended with the Grate Fire of London and the Restoration of Charles II (Bonnie Prince Charlie), whose coronation was greeted with shouts of applause in Pepys' *Dairy* and throughout London. With the Carolingian

Period officially commenced the Age of Innocents Abroad, during which the English court became decidedly French and therefore wicked. France was then in her Golden Age under Louis D'Or, also known as the Prodigal Sun. Pleased with this state of extreme culture, Charles introduced into England such French innovations as Neo-Chasticism, the Bucolic Plague and champagne at tea.

To Charles' loose morals Nell Gwyn, a clown in Piccadilly Circus, was only the natural accompaniment. This ravishing creature was, roughly speaking, the positive symposium of pulchritude, and in addition she featured one of the most beautiful rhyme schemes in English literature. Even her participles dangled. It would, of course, have been virtuously impossible for Charles to marry this loose liver, for she was decidedly a woman of the wrong world. In his hands the thing became a strumpet.

Shortly thereafter England decomposed Charles II and invited William the Silent to the British throne. William gladly accepted England's invitation (the Overture to the Flying Dutchman) and, once in London, promptly

THE BUCOLIC PLAGUE
Pepys' Dairy in the Foreground
From an Old Print Now in the Flatbush Archive

passed the so-called Glorious Resolution, according to which: (1) no man might be beheaded without his own consent; (2) no king could order taxis without permission from Parliament; and (3) England would henceforth be a limited mockery.

CHAPTER SIX

The Great Wolf

Hic sex rex.
—Virgil

At the coronation of Anne Boleyn in 1702 John Dryden honored her assent to the throne with an exquisite rime royal entitled *Anna Mirabile,* a coronach celebrating the domestic virtues of the new monarch. Thereupon Queen Anne officially inaugurated the Age of Popes and Swifts, and peace and prosperity raged throughout the island for more than a decade. English culture was at last *ruse in urbe.* Antiques were plentiful and mistresses were quite common. Frequently such men of fashion as Beau Brummel, Beau Geste and Beau Stratagem congregated for chocolate and

A SUNDAY IN THE COUNTRY WITH
SIR ROGER DE COVERLET

Beau Geste covers his face with his hand. The custom depicted here dates from the Old Anguische tradition and was resuscitated by men of fashion in the eighteenth century.
Chocolate was served afterward.

From a print hanging in Will Coffin House

politics at Will's Coffin-House or spent a Sunday in the country with Sir Roger de Coverlet. It was indeed England's Golden Age *par excellence.*

To commemorate the accession of George I and the House of Hangover in 1714, Alexander Pope translated Virgil's *Georgics* and wrote an epistle to Dr. Arbuthnot. For centuries Latin literature had been a source of unspeakable satisfaction to millions, and Pope established the Neo-Classical School in London to perpetrate Rome's legacy to Western civilization. Although the school was frequently closed for altercations, such ancient classics as Polonius, Calculus and Livid were held in high esteem. In his translations Pope labored to immortalize also the works of Leviticus, Parnassus, Octopus and Marius the Epicurean.

Pope has been called "the high priest of an Age of Pose and Reason." While still in infancy his parents read to him the complete works of Shakespeare, Milton and Wordsworth, and as a child he composed such bits of light society verse as "The Ill-Tempered Clavichord" and "My Bonnet Lies over the Ocean; or, The Teapot

Dome." Eventually he translated Homer's *Idiot* and *Oddity* into impeccable heroic cutlets.

In 1712 Jacob Tonson published Locke's *Rape of the Pope,* a satire relating the melancholy story of a flirt whose coiffure was ruthlessly disheveled during a card game at Hampton Roads. Although this piece was little more than a frank *tour de farce,* Pope construed Locke's poem as a personal affront (the Popish Plot) and retaliated in his didactyllic "Peri-Bathos; or, The Art of Stinking in Poetry," another bit of light society verse, now preserved in the Vacuum at Rome. Some critics consider Pope pedestrian because he wrote only in iambic feet, but of all English poets he is probably the most distinguished for polish and wit.

Parody and burlesque dominated Augustan England. In *Treasure Ireland,* a novel based on Mandeville's *Fable of the Birds and the Bees,* Jonathan Swift proved that burlesque has a broad meaning, usually involving a take-off of some kind. In similar spirit William Hogarth depicted the human comedy in "The Rape's Progress," generally known as "The Prints Charming." Finally

John Gay's *Burglar's Opera* burlesqued Macbeth, a notorious highwayman whose wife dies of sleeping sickness in Act V.

Through Henry Fielding's efforts the Licensing Act of 1737 provided that all broadsides be censured by the government. It was Samuel Richardson's *Pamela; or, Virgin Rewarded,* an expostulary novel, that first brought this law into action. Richardson later published *Sir Charles' Grandson; or, Female Difficulties* and *Clarissa Harlot; or, The Mistakes of a Night.* Eventually Laurence Sterne, the Little Minister, purified the tone of fiction in *Tristram Shanty.* Fielding, of course, had already paved the way in *Amelia; or, A Lady in Waiting.*

Neo-Chasticism witnessed also the rise of periodical literature. Some of the most conspicuous literary creations of Augustan England first appeared on the pages of *The Harlem Miscellany* and *The Ladies' Monthly.* In 1709 Addison Steele commenced the *Tatler* and *Spectator* papers, semiweakly periodicals reporting births, deaths, marriages and other public calamities. Aiming to "bring philology out of the clouds into clubs and

ANCIENT EGYPTIAN HYDRAULIC FOUND
ON ONE OF THE PYRENEES

coffin-houses," Steele published hundreds of familiar essays from which *The New Yorker* can trace direct dissent.

At last Steele died of Addison's disease, but his work was carried on by Lady Mary Worthless Montagu, an eighteenth-century millionheiress whose celebrated *Tour de Force* describes her travels in blue stockings in the Near East. In Alexandria Mrs. Montagu met Rosetta Stone, an early archaeologist, who provided her a key to the ancient Egyptian hydraulics on the Sphinx and Pyrenees.

It was through Mrs. Montagu's introduction that Sir Horace Walpole, longest prime minister of England, began his distinguished correspondence with Lady Charlotte Russe of Moscow. Walpole lived on Raspberry Hill, an ancient Gothic ruin near Heathcliff. He studied for some years at Sheridan's School, whence he wrote his well-known *Letter from So Ho, a Citizen of the World, to His Friend Ching-Ching the Chinaman.*

England's interest in orientalism had commenced with Adam Smith's *Wealth of Natives* early in the eighteenth century. Thereafter, London was invaded by such famous orientals as

Formosa and Mimosa, Fling Woo and Water Loo, and scores of others too humorous to mention. Through the good offices of Mikado, London emissary of the Japanese Shotgun, Pajama introduced to London drawing rooms his wife Kimono, whom Boswell found to be an extraordinary example of "soft" primitivism. Later a sharp contrast between oriental and accidental culture became apparent when Sing Sing, formerly known as Sing Sang Sung, introduced to Englishmen the philosophy of Buddha the Pest, and when Hegira, wife of Mohammed, published the *Korean* at the suggestion of the Hindu Marjoram.

CHAPTER SEVEN

The Wolf in Street Clothing

Le style c'est moi.
—Dr. Johnson

For half a century Dr. Ben Johnson, Prince of Whales, figured very largely in London as the literary dictator of Augustan England. Even as a child he went to Juvenal Court to answer charges brought against his satires. Later he wrote Lord Chesterton's *Dictionary*, and in 1763 he met Boswell, who forthwith devoted himself to Johnson's career.

To Johnson it was a joy to breathe the Londonderry air. When he was not sharing a bottle of champagne with the Countess of Pembroke on Quality Street, he was enjoying a chat with

Mrs. Thrale over tea and strumpets on Back Street, or consuming Cheshire cheese with his daughter Irene at the Bore's Head Tavern on Fleet Street. Johnson made many fast friends in London, among the fastest being Dr. Burney, father of Fanny Brice, and Edward Gibbon, whose *Decline and Fall* Fanny Brice said was neither Empire nor Chippendale.

Meanwhile English Neo-Chasticism had gone from bad to worst. One Thomas Gray (whose aunt, Lucy Gray, was a cousin of Wordsworth on his maternal side) had visited a romantic churchyard at Stoke Penge, where he had produced his famous "Allergy Written in a Country Churchyard," beginning: "The curfew shall not ring tonight." Inspired by her classic mews, Gray then wrote "An Ode on the Death of a Favorite Catfish Drowned in a Tub of Goldfinches." At his death Dr. Johnson composed Gray's Elegy for the occasion, and even today tourists at Stoke Penge may see Gray's effigy in the country churchyard.

Shortly thereafter the romantic precurser Edward Young attended the Graveyard School in the City of Dreadful Night, where he wrote his well-known thousand and one *Night Thoughts,* most famous of which are "The Twelfth Night" and "The Night Before Christmas." Later Thomas Percy inaugurated the Antiquarian Movement with his memorable *Reliques of Ancient Poultry,* which promptly inspired the forgeries of James Macpherson and Thomas Chatterton. Macpherson, the Old Pretender, first wrote *Ossian* and then produced *Fragments of Ancient Pottery,* a study of ceramic art in Fingal's Cave. Although no one knew at first whether Ossian was alive and composing or dead and decomposing, Dr. Johnson finally proved that the poems were spurious and that *Fingal's Cave* was actually the work of Felix Mendelssohn.

Later Thomas Chatterton was named the Young Pretender when his *Rowdey Poems* (the Purloined Letters) were published under false pretenses. Following his marriage to a Miss Fortune this "Marvelous Boy," fed up with having nothing to eat, died of suicide.

Poverty was also the lot of Robert Burns, known today chiefly for his treatment *Of Mice and Women.* The son of a coal minor, Burns revealed his uncommon love for uncommon animals in "To a Mouse," "To a Louse" and "To a Grouse."

Already Sir Walter Raleigh's *Lay of the Last Minister,* an attack on clerical immorality, had inspired such novelists as Henry Brooke (the fool of quality), Henry Mackenzie (the man of feeling) and Ann Gothica Radcliffe (the bride of Frankenstein). Mrs. Radcliffe was born in the Castle of Otranto on Lake Eerie. After reading Sir Horace Walpole's *Castle of Othello* she introduced the adventures of Shylock Holmes into *The Mistress of Udolpho.* Certainly Mrs. Radcliffe is more to be pitied than censored, but Lady Jane Austen censored Mrs. Radcliffe freely in the vitreous humor of her celebrated novel of manors, *Prudes and Prudence.*

CHAPTER EIGHT

The Warp and the Wolf

He who laughs least lasts best.
—Shakespeare

With the publication of *Lyrical Ballast* William Wordsworth assumed the chief position in English letters formally held by Dr. Johnson. Born in London, Wordsworth spent his childhood near the Great Lakes, among the Wigglesworths, Wordsworths and Woolworths of Wordsworthshire. Later he attended Maudlin College, Oxford, where he invented perpetual emotion in his "Lines Composed near Northanger Abbey." Flowers violently affected a man of Wordsworth's constituency—especially cauliflowers, dactyls and nevergreens—and even the meanest flower that

PERPETUAL EMOTION
Northanger Abbey in the background. The suppliant figure is presumably a Wigglesworth.

From an Engraving now in the Hands of Lord Cholmondeley, Bert.

blows brought him thoughts which lay, fortunately, too deep for tears. Following his marriage he assumed the name of "Daddy Wordsworth" and speedily became one of England's most prolific writers.

Wordsworth frequently wrote poems and prefaces, and sometimes he wrote literature. His most famous mistake appeared in "The Solitary Raper," composed by the seaside near Cathay: "The child," he wrote, "is the father of the man." He was particularly proud of his "Ode on Imitations of Immorality from Regulations of Early Childhood," in which he maintained that rural life is found chiefly in the country. His pathetic fallacy was, of course, his persistence in writing poetry after his inspiration had ceased.

It was Wordsworth's co-evil, Samuel Taylor Coleridge, who first opposed the enthusiasm for common life shown in *Lyrical Ballast.* Coleridge was also one of the first to appreciate Shakespearean drama, and his *Caricatures of Shakespeare's Plays* remains today as definitive as Lamb's *Twice-Told Tales.* His greatest poem is "The Ancient Mariner," the moral of which, as stated by Silas the Mariner, is simply: "Obey the Fish and Game Laws." In *The Road to Timbuktu* John Livingston Lowes suggested that the key to this poem lies in Widener Library.

William Jennings Byron, author of "Thanatopsis," is considered "the playboy of the western world." As a child he was called Harold, but at school he became known as the Wolf. At Harrow he played Rugby, served on the tennis team and gambled on the village green with Bella Donna, an Italian lady of English distraction. Finally he married his first cousin, and the belles of London peeled forth. After that first fine careless rupture, however, the Byrons moved from Bond Street to Tobacco Road, where Lord Byron lived amid all the unadulterated lust practicable in a private household. On the morning after the appearance of *English Birds and Scotch Retrievers* he awoke to find himself, but was disappointed. Later he was exiled to Don Juan, whence he finally escaped to Greece. In Athens he visited the Palace Athena, the Pantheon and the Apocalypse, and there, amid the throws of a wild and wolfy love affair, he was inspired to compose "Childe Harold to the Dark Tower Came." After numerous touching scenes he died in the Battle

WILLIAM JENNINGS BYRON
Author of *Thanatopsis*
From the Original Portrait by Lady Zane Grey now in the Possession of Edward Lord Brute

of Marathon. Psychiatrists now believe that Byron suffered from lycanthropy, according to which one is cracked (symmetrically) and imagines himself to be and acts like a wolf. Certainly his sounding brass and tinkling symbols reveal a man less sinned against than sinning, but he was probably a good man underneath. His poetry contains overtones (and undertones) embracing all mankind—especially persons of the opposite sex.

Most fragile of all romantic poets was Percy Bysshe Shelley, a victim of abnormal psychology, whom Benedict Arnold once called "an ineffective Anglican flapping his lunatic wings in the void." Shelley's poetry may be termed "strictly platonic," but his private life found best expression in *Promiscuous Unbound,* a tragedy based on the philosophy of Plato and Isosceles. His belief in Pantherism first appeared in "Adenoids," a lament for Keats based on Byron's "Lament for Adonais." Unfortunately Shelley died while drowning in the Bay of Spumoni. A simple epithet marks his tomb: "Here lies one whose fame was writ in water."

In his "Ode on a Greasy Urn" John Keats proved himself the most sensual poet in the language. At twenty-five he married a musician named Agnes Dei, and on top of that he met a speedy death from tuberoses. Keats' wife inspired "The Keats of St. Agnes," a narrative poem dedicated to Calliope, Errata and Uranium. But his greatest contribution to English literature is his "Ode to Madame Nightingale," addressed to the famous French opera singer who, filled with the milk of human kindness, nursed to health the British soldiers of the Crimean War.

CHAPTER NINE

Dyed in the Wolf

Any poet in a storm.
—Dr. Johnson

In 1837 George III died of a cerebral hemorrhoid, and Queen Victoria, though asleep at the time, immediately ascended the English throne. Thereafter for more than fifty years England lived in the "splendid oscillation" of her ivory tower. Under Lord George the Corn Laws were declared dull and void, and England began to manufacture iron and steal. During the Bore War Rudyard Kipling crystallized British imperialism in his classic *Wee Winnie Winkle; or, The Last Days of Bombay.* Finally, at the celebration of Victoria's Diamond Jubilee in 1897, an invested choir of two thousand vices performed "Anchors Away" before Queen Victoria and Lord Tweedsuit under the vast unsupported roof of the Crystal Palace.

An early Victorious prose writer of considerable prominence was Thomas Carlyle, a Scotchman whose wife, Jane Carlyle, was Welsh. Carlyle was Professor of Things in General at the University of Teufelsdröckh. He was also an intimate friend of Ralph Walden Thoreau, pastor of First Utilitarian Church in Boston. Famous for his self-reliance, Thoreau founded the Transmigration Movement and preached the transmutation of souls, according to which God speaks to Transmigrationists through transoms.

It was this movement that prompted John Henry Newman to publish *Masses from an Old Manse.* Here Newman explained how, as a friend of Pope Interdict XII, he sold his manse, became a cardinal and wrote "Lead Kindly Light." About this time Charles Darwin, Aldous Huxley's bulldog, announced his theory of evolution, according to which "ontology recapitulates philology." Thereupon Cardinal Newman fiercely denounced Darwin from every pulpit in England. At once

Huxley rose to Darwin's defense in *Point Counterpoint,* a text on musical theory, and Walter Horatio Pater, one of the sons of Baliol, proved himself the father of the Aesthetic Movement by calling Newman "a child in the house."

Victorious England also boasted a Dickens, a Thackeray, an Eliot and a Trollope. In the hands of these "imminent Victorians" English fiction grew by leaps and bounds, and with the appearance of Dickens' *Nicholas Nickleby,* the first cut-rate dime novel, English fiction at last came of age. In *Vanity Fair* William Masterpiece Thackeray, editor of *Blockhead's Magazine,* reintroduced into fiction the English humors of the eighteenth century. Less of a classicist was George Fielding Eliot, whose *Ramona,* a tale of Savonaromola, foreshadowed *Scenes from Clerical Life,* an exposé of London office conditions.

In his imaginary conversations Walter Savage Landor, "the grandest old Romeo of them all," stimulated an interest in classical iniquity which found notable expression in the verse of Tennyson and Browning. Throughout the work of these two poets one observes numerous allusions to such familiar myths as Juno and the Peacock, Cyclone

FLUSH
Wife of Robert Browning
Shown against a Background of Ravioli and Blanc Mange
From the Original Portrait by Fra Michael Angelico now in the Possession of Angelina Torso

and the Doldrums, Amoeba and the Myriads, and Orpheus and Euripides.

Unlike most poets, Alfred Lloyd Tennyson neither smoked, drank nor took poison. In early youth he published "Crossing the Bar," a poem on the legal aspects of death in the form of a tribute to the Anti-Saloon League. Seeking some momentum of his deceased friend Author Hallam, Tennyson wrote *In Memorandum* to perpetuate the death of Hallam while drowning across Lake Windermere in 1850. Robert Browning was so moved by this poem's expiring religious message that he produced a dramatic monologue entitled *Sordido,* which he later presented to his wife Flush, whose less-than-kind father then lived on Barrett Street near Berkeley Square. On their honeymoon the Brownings visited Rome, Larghetto and Naples, after which they settled in Ravioli near Blanc Mange, where Browning composed a toccata at Galuppi's and wrote the libretto for Wagner's *Ring of the Nibelung.*

CHAPTER TEN

Cry Woolf!

Snap back with Steinbeck.
—Contemptuary Slogan

At the end of Victoria's reign cultural affairs were at high tide. Strindberg's *Peter and the Wolf* had inspired the discords of Stravinsky's *Firecracker Suite,* and Henri Métisse had discovered Modern Art at the Local Color School in Paris. John Greenleaf Whistler had painted his mother; George Bernard Shaw had translated Voltaire's *Candide;* and Arthur Wing Pirandello had shocked Covent Garden with *Sex Characters in Search of an Author.* In London the Wilde Nineties officially commenced with the composition of "The Merry Widow Waltz" and

AUDREY BEARDSLEY
Marquess of Middlesex
From the Original Portrait by Cecil Beaton. Now in the Possession of the Countess of Boorfield

the publication of Henry James' *Aspirin Papers.*

Like all great dramatists Oscar Wilde was Irish and always loved the Irish Free State. Actually, however, his ancestors were from Bohemia, and he himself eventually settled near his friend Audrey Beardsley in Middlesex. At Oxford, Wilde scandalized the British Empire with his infamous *Picture of Duncan Gray.* And when *Salomé and Delilah* was first sung before a British audience by Gloria Swansong, even Queen Victoria shouted "Paris forbid!" and promptly quitted the theater. Accused of vice versa, Wilde was immediately sent to Coventry, a rotten borough, where he published *A Ballad Read in Jail.*

Wilde's plays were produced by Sir Max Beerbohm Tree, who also encouraged other dramatists of "The English Pail" to follow the footsteps of Synge's *Riders to the Sea.* Accordingly such Irish playwrights as O'Casey, O'Neill and O'Henry studied the theories of Sigmund Fraud, analyzed the works of Maxim Gawky, and turned for inspiration to Ibsen's *Ugly Duckling.*

Meanwhile Modern Poetry had begun in 1857 with the publication of Walt Whitman's

Blades of Grass, a volume which introduced the use of free verse in English. Free verse is verse without rhyme or reason, as in Whitman's lines from "Psalm of Myself":

> I contradict myself?
> I contradict myself
> Very well.

This passage requires no comment. Following Whitman's free-verse tradition, Stephen Hart Crane, brother of Ichabod Crane, felt encouraged to produce even more radical departures from commonly excepted tradition and jumped off a boat, to be later commemorated by Imagist revolutionaries who cried, "A poem is like a mute fruit!"

Those who keep abreast of the *Times* know that the field of modern fiction is hopelessly vast and complex. Such critics as Louis Academic and Bernard de Veto observe freudulent tendencies in the contemptuary novel, while others re-echo the defeatism of Spengler's *Decline of Mae West*. In the late nineteenth century William James, Henry James and Jesse James upset American literature by becoming neutralized British citizens, and it was not until World War I that returning veteranarians fused new blood into contemptuary spirit. Any list of significant modern novelists must include such names as Matthew Arnold Bennett, John Erskine Caldwell and Upton Sinclair Lewis, whose well-known *Arrowshirt* exposed Irving Babbitt and shaped the course of English friction.

At present, of course, the greatest English wolf is Virginia Woolf, who employed the "scream-of-consciousness" technique in *Mrs. Dashaway* and *Rum of One's Own.* Although she distinctly preferred novels to fiction, Mrs. Woolf made substantial contributions in both fields and performed the vital function of bringing modern fiction to its present state of eloquence. And, unless something very foreseen occurs, it is probable that English literature will continue to flourish until the last syllabus of recorded time.